FASTBACK ® Crime and Detection

Beginner's Luck

RICHARD LAYMON

GLOBE FEARON
Pearson Learning Group

FASTBACK® CRIME AND DETECTION BOOKS

Beginner's Luck
The Blind Alley
Fun World
The Kid Who Sold Money
The Lottery Winner

No Loose Ends
Return Payment
The Setup
Small-Town Beat
Snowbound

Cover *t.r.* Eyewire/Getty Images, Inc.; *m.* Sami Sarkis/Getty Images, Inc. All photography © Pearson Education, Inc. (PEI) unless specifically noted.

Copyright © 2004 by Pearson Education, Inc., publishing as Globe Fearon®, an imprint of Pearson Learning Group, 299 Jefferson Road, Parsippany, NJ 07054. All rights reserved. No part of this book may be reproduced or transmitted in any form or by any means, electronic or mechanical, including photocopying, recording, or by any information storage and retrieval system, without permission in writing from the publisher. For information regarding permission(s), write to Rights and Permissions Department.

Globe Fearon® and Fastback® are registered trademarks of Globe Fearon, Inc.

ISBN 0-13-024489-9
Printed in the United States of America
1 2 3 4 5 6 7 8 9 10   07 06 05 04 03

1-800-321-3106
www.pearsonlearning.com

"Five?" asked the bookstore clerk when Joyce set the copies of *Whispering Shadows Mystery Monthly* on the counter.

"I have a story in it," Joyce told her. She felt a blush spread over her cheeks as she smiled.

"Really? How exciting!"

"It's my second story. I sold my first to them a few months ago."

The clerk, a young woman who seemed to be about Joyce's age of 19, opened one of the magazines. She moved her finger down the table of contents page, along the list of authors. She stopped at Joyce's name. "I bet you're Joyce Walther," she said.

Joyce beamed. "Right! How did you know?"

"Elementary, my dear Watson. I'm a fan of this magazine. I read your first story when it came out. It was very good, by the way. At the time, your name stuck in my mind, because the introduction said you live here in town. And I've also been to your father's store." Grinning, she swept back some wavy brown hair and showed a gold earring to Joyce. "Then, of course, you were in the news for the way you caught those thugs. With all that, how *could* I forget your name?"

Joyce shook her head, amazed. "You'd make a good detective," she said.

No other customers were waiting, so the clerk hurried to the magazine rack. She rushed back to the counter with another copy. "How about an autograph?" she asked. "Make it to Susie."

Delighted, Joyce turned to page 63. Just below her printed name, she scribbled, "For Susie, a real Sherlock Holmes. All my best, Joyce Walther."

"Oh, this is great," Susie said as she read what Joyce had written.

"I hope you like the story," Joyce told her.

"If it's half as good as the first one, I'm sure I will. You've got real talent. And you're a heroine, too."

Joyce was still blushing with pleasure when she finished paying for her magazines and left the bookstore. Turning to the right, she headed down the wide, crowded aisle of the shopping mall. At the far end was another bookstore. She was going to stop there to buy a few more copies of the magazine. Later, she planned to drive all over Santa Monica to buy a lot more.

The magazine's publisher had given her the usual number of copies an author gets—three. But she needed at least 15 just for relatives and friends. And she wanted 15 or 20 more to keep for herself. "You can't have too many," she thought. "They'll be almost impossible to get, once the next issue hits the stands."

"Excuse me, miss," a voice said, interrupting her thoughts.

She turned her head to look at the young man suddenly walking beside her. He was handsome, with blond curly hair and a pleasant smile. His tan jacket was buttoned over a sport shirt.

"Yes?" she said.

"Do you have a blue Ford parked on level one of the mall lot?" He glanced at a scrap of paper in his hand. "License plate 633 TME?"

Joyce's stomach knotted. "Yes, I do," she said. "Why?"

"My partner and I spotted a prowler. We think he broke into your car."

Joyce suddenly felt sick as she stared at the young man. "Did he take anything?" she asked.

"We're not sure. We spotted him just as he was running away. My partner went after him, and I came to look for you."

"How did you know that I was the one driving that car?" Joyce asked.

He shook his head. "It wasn't easy finding you. There was a woman who saw what was going on. She told me that she'd parked near you and saw you get out. She described you. Unfortunately, this mall seems to be full of young women with blond hair who are wearing plaid skirts. I checked with seven or eight before I got to you. Now, if you don't mind, I'd like you to come along with me. We'll take a look in your car and see if he stole any of your property."

"OK," Joyce said. They walked across the mall.

"By the way, I'm Officer Stevens, Santa Monica Police Department. What's your name?"

"Joyce Walther," she answered. For a moment she was disappointed that he didn't seem to recognize her name. "Don't be silly," she told herself. "It's been six months since you helped catch those thieves. You can hardly expect every member of the police force to remember you."

"Did you have any valuables in the car?" he asked.

"I sure did. My dad's binoculars and camera were under the driver's seat." She remembered her father laughing when she'd asked to borrow them. "Let me guess," her father had said. "You want them handy just in case you run into a crime." She had admitted it, and they had both laughed. As it turned out, however, Joyce could've done without the binoculars and camera. All the time she'd been carrying them around, she hadn't even used them once. "Some detective," she thought. "I should have left Dad's gear safe at home."

"The thief," she asked. "Was he carrying anything?"

"He appeared to have objects hidden under his jacket."

"Oh, man," she muttered.

At the end of the corridor, Officer Stevens pushed open the glass door and held it for Joyce. They entered the parking area.

"Maybe we'll be in luck, Joyce. My partner's quick on his feet. He probably chased down the suspect."

"I sure hope he did."

They crossed the lane and walked past the rear bumpers of parked cars. Joyce's car was still out of sight, around the bend. But she scanned what she could see of the lot, looking for Stevens's partner. The few people she saw all looked like shoppers, either on their way into the mall or out.

Stevens grabbed Joyce's arm and yanked her out of danger as a station wagon backed up. Its rear bumper brushed the front of her skirt.

"Hey!" Stevens pounded its roof with his open hand. The car jerked to a stop. Bending over, he peered through the open passenger window. The tail end of his jacket slid up. Below its hem, Joyce saw a gleaming curve of metal—a rim of his handcuffs. "You almost ran this young lady down," Stevens told the driver in a stern voice. "I ought to run you in for reckless driving.

But I have more important matters to deal with. In the future, be more careful."

"Yes, sir," the driver said, sounding frightened.

"Be on your way," Stevens ordered as he stepped back to let the car finish pulling out. He turned to Joyce. "Are you all right?"

"I'm fine," she said. "Thanks for stopping me."

"My pleasure," he said. Smiling, he patted her arm. "You'd better watch where you're walking," he warned in a gentle voice. "I'd hate for anything bad to happen to a young lady as pretty as you."

His compliment, plus the way he'd patted her arm, made Joyce uncomfortable. He was being a little too friendly for a police officer, she thought. But he had, after all, just saved her from possibly being hit by a car. Because of that, maybe he felt especially protective.

When they rounded the turn in the lane, she looked up and spotted her car. She half expected to find Stevens's partner standing near it, the suspect in custody. Instead there wasn't anybody there.

"Where's your partner?" she asked.

Frowning, Stevens shook his head. He didn't answer right away. As they walked toward her car, he finally answered, "Do you know what probably happened? Rick must've caught him. I can't imagine *anyone* getting away from Rick—he was a star sprinter in college. He must have caught the suspect and taken him in."

"To the police station?" Joyce asked.

"That's probably just what he did." Shaking his head as if amused by his partner, he said, "Rick's a real hot dog. He probably hauled the guy in, all by himself. Then he wouldn't have to share the collar with me."

"Doesn't that make you mad?" Joyce asked.

Stevens shrugged, then smiled in a carefree way. "I'm an easygoing guy. It takes a lot to make me mad."

They stopped beside Joyce's car. She was glad to see that none of its windows were broken. The lock buttons all appeared to be in the down position. She sighed with relief. "It doesn't look like he got in."

"We'd better make sure," Stevens said.

Joyce took the key case from her purse.

"Let me," he told her. She gave the leather case to him. Choosing the right key, he slid it into the door, turned it, and pulled the handle.

Joyce hissed through her teeth.

"What?" he asked, looking over his shoulder.

"Nothing," she said. "I'm just a little nervous."

"If he did get in, you probably just loused up his fingerprints," she thought. But she didn't say it because she didn't want to embarrass him.

Stevens ducked low and slid a hand under the driver's seat. He straightened up slowly, shook his head, and turned to Joyce. "Nothing there," he said. "I'm afraid he got the camera and binoculars. He probably got in using a coat hanger to flip up the lock button. But don't worry. I'd bet a month's pay that Rick has the guy safely behind bars by now."

"I sure hope so," Joyce said.

"My van's just over there." He nodded toward a row of cars parked across the lane. "I'll take you over to the station. If we're in luck, your dad's equipment will be there and you can fill out a complaint against the suspect."

"If the suspect is there," Joyce said, feeling discouraged.

"Don't worry, he will be."

Joyce followed him as he stepped between a nice, shiny car and a beat-up green van. The van had a broken tail light, a Nevada license plate, and a crumpled side panel.

Stevens opened the van's passenger door.

Joyce stopped. "This is yours?"

He gave her a sheepish smile. "Kind of a mess, isn't it? We use it for undercover work."

"If this is your van," she asked, "how did Rick take the thief to the station?"

"In his car. We meet here sometimes because this mall is a lot closer to Rick's apartment than the station." Stevens's smile turned bright. "What's going on inside that pretty little head of yours?"

Joyce took a deep breath. She was getting very nervous. She didn't want to seem rude, but something about all this wasn't quite right. Rubbing her sweaty hands on her skirt, she said, "Would you mind showing me some identification?"

"**I** don't mind at all," he said. But it was plain from the look in his eyes that he felt insulted by Joyce's request. As he reached toward a back pocket of his trousers, his hand swept his jacket open and Joyce saw his gun. It was holstered at his left hip, its handle forward for a cross-draw. It had the flat grips of a semiautomatic, and she spotted the base of its ammo magazine before his jacket fell back to cover it.

Swinging his hand toward Joyce, he opened his wallet. She caught a glimpse of a gold star before he flipped the wallet shut. "OK?" he asked.

"Fine," Joyce said. She managed a shaky smile. "For a minute there, I was starting to wonder."

"Well, I can't blame you for being careful. You've probably been warned, all your life, about talking to strangers."

"Policemen don't count as strangers," Joyce said. She climbed into the van and sat down on the torn passenger seat.

Stevens shut the door for her. He walked around to the other side, opened his door, and got in behind the steering wheel. He turned the ignition key, and the engine started right away.

"This sure messes up my day," she said as they pulled away. "I was planning to hit about a dozen more bookstores."

"Oh?" he said, steering slowly down the lane of the parking lot.

"Yes," Joyce told him. "I have a mystery story in a magazine that just came out."

"You're a writer?" he asked.

"That's right. I've sold two stories, so far. Are you sure you haven't heard of me? Joyce Walther?"

"I don't read much," he admitted.

"Well, I helped the department a few months ago. They even gave me a special award. I helped catch a couple of guys."

Stevens glanced at Joyce and raised his eyebrows. "Oh, sure I remember. Joyce Walther. You were the talk of the department."

She nodded. "One guy held my mom and me hostage while his partner forced my dad to take him to the coin shop. He was after Dad's rare coins, you know."

"Sure, I remember now."

"I'm kind of an amateur detective. I'm really fascinated by police work."

Stevens gave her a stern look. "You should leave police work to the professionals. It can get dangerous, you know."

"I can take care of myself," Joyce told him. She hoped she was right.

In silence, she stared out the dirty windshield. She squinted against the sunlight as the van eased out of the lot and began moving up the street.

"If I *can't* take care of myself," she thought, "I'm in big trouble. Because the man behind the wheel of this van is not a police officer."

She had first started to wonder about him when he opened her car door. He hadn't made any attempt to preserve any fingerprints that the suspect might have left on the handle. It could have been carelessness, though. From her vast reading of true crime books, she knew that police officers sometimes botch up evidence.

The battered green van, however, with its broken tail light and Nevada license plate, had set off an alarm in her mind.

At that point, she had wanted to see his identification and get a look at his handgun. She knew that regulation issue for the department was a .38-caliber revolver. This guy was carrying a semiautomatic. But plainclothes officers might be allowed to carry the weapon of their choice. She just wasn't sure about that.

She *was* sure about his badge. It looked like a Los Angeles County Sheriff's Office star, not the shield of the Santa Monica Police Department. Stevens had claimed to be with the police department. His quick flash of the wrong badge had changed Joyce's suspicions into a dark certainty.

For a final test, she had led him into the story of her capturing the thieves. "Sure," he'd said, "now I remember." If he truly remembered the case, however, he would have known that the two men had not been after rare coins. Her father owned a jewelry store, not a coin shop. The evidence was all against him.

He wasn't a cop. More than likely, he'd been inside his van when Joyce drove into her parking place. And he'd seen her climb out. That's how he matched her up with her car. He hadn't seen any prowler. He didn't have a partner. "In fact," Joyce thought with some relief, "the camera and binoculars are probably still under the seat." She had only his word that they'd been stolen. And he was lying about everything else. That, she supposed, was the cloud's silver lining.

Not a lot to cheer about.

Not when you're riding through downtown Santa Monica with a kidnapper—or worse.

Joyce felt herself start to panic. "Calm down," she thought. "If you fall to pieces, he'll know you're onto him. So far, you've got him fooled."

"I might become a policewoman," she said, breaking the silence. "I've been taking some police science courses in college. They're research for my writing, you know, but I should probably have some kind of job in case I can't make a living as an author." She was pleased that her voice sounded steady.

"Good idea," Stevens said. He turned right.

"Could I have a look at your side arm?" she asked.

He looked at Joyce as if he thought she had lost her mind.

"I'll be careful," she said.

"It's against regulations," he said.

"You're good," Joyce thought. "But not good enough."

She hadn't really expected Stevens to hand the gun to her. But it had been worth a try.

After stopping at a traffic light, he picked up speed crossing the intersection. Joyce guessed he was doing 20 miles an hour in the curb lane when she swung up her right hand. The bag in her grip, loaded with the five magazines, whapped him solidly on the nose. Stevens yelped with surprise. Twisting in her seat, Joyce used her other hand to tug the steering wheel. The van lurched to the right and bounded over the curb. She threw herself against the door, jerked its handle, and tumbled out.

She seemed to fall for a long time. Her shoulder hit the sidewalk. She cried out in pain and clutched her head as she tumbled over the concrete. She was still rolling when she heard the loud crash of the van.

She staggered to her feet. The van had smashed right into the wall of a bank.

A security guard came running out of the bank door, a hand on his holstered pistol.

"Draw it!" Joyce yelled to the guard. "He's got a gun! He kidnapped me!"

Scowling, the bank guard drew his revolver and ran toward the van.

Joyce followed, staying some distance behind him.

She watched the guard shove his weapon into the driver's window. Then, stepping back, he pulled open the door. Stevens fell to the sidewalk and didn't move.

"You're quite a young woman," said Lt. Harold Cameron at police headquarters. "The FBI has been trying to nail Morgan for months. That's his real name, Jack Morgan. He's wanted for a whole string of kidnappings. He just picked his victims at random. Then he'd hold them prisoner in his van until he got his hands on the ransom money."

"That doesn't seem to be any way to make a haul," Joyce said. "You want to pick wealthy victims, and. . . ."

"He thought he was being very smart. He figured he would bring down too much heat if he tried for a huge take. So instead he settled for a lot of small ones. And the method worked just fine until you came along."

"I'm glad I could help," Joyce said. "I knew he wasn't up to any good. I mean, some guy pretending to be a police officer. . . ."

"You said that you had your doubts about him before you got into his van. Why on earth did you go along with him?"

"I didn't think my chances would be

very good if I tried to make a run for it inside the parking lot. Remember, I'd seen his gun. I didn't want to get shot. I figured that I'd have a better chance if I could make him crash somewhere along a busy street. I didn't buckle my seat belt when I got in the van. I thought that would make it easier for me to jump clear if we crashed. Then, when I saw that we were going past a bank. . . ."

"You took a terrible risk," Lieutenant Cameron said.

Joyce shrugged, as if it were nothing. "I can take care of myself," she said.

"Those were probably the famous last words of a thousand victims, Miss Walther."

Her smile slipped just a bit. "Well," she said, "it turned out all right."

"This time."

"Don't worry," she said. "After this, I won't trust anyone—not even anyone wearing a uniform and sitting behind a desk at a police headquarters. By the way, do you have some identification?"

Lieutenant Cameron laughed. "Now you're talking," he said, reaching for his wallet.

RICHARD LAYMON*'s speciality is writing horror tales. He is the author of the best-selling book* The Cellar *and several other horror and suspense novels.*